PRESENTED TO

Joanna

BY

Nancy Bartola

DATE

_2-24-09_

JOYCE ROGERS

GRACE

for the

WIDOW

A JOURNEY THROUGH THE FOG OF LOSS

B&H
PUBLISHING GROUP
Nashville, Tennessee

978-0-8054-4846-7

Published by B&H Publishing Group
Nashville, Tennessee

Dewey Decimal Classification: 248.86
Subject Heading: BEREAVEMENT \ GRIEF \
WIDOWS—LIFE SKILLS GUIDES

1 2 3 4 5 6 7 8 • 13 12 11 10 09

DEDICATION

I dedicate this book to my "Beloved"—Adrian Rogers—whom I have loved since I was but a child. He was filled with love, wisdom, courage, and integrity. I miss him greatly, but I rejoice that he can be with the One he loved so much.

Adrian invited multitudes to "come to Jesus." I invite you now to "come to Jesus" with your burdens and sorrows. If you don't know Jesus personally, surrender your all to Him today.

ACKNOWLEDGMENTS

I want to give thanks to all those who helped bring this book to fruition.

Thanks first of all to my Lord and Savior, Jesus Christ, Who has sustained me in my darkest hour of grief and brought me through the "fog of loss." He is there for me every day and has given me hope for my tomorrows.

Thanks to Thomas Walters at B&H Publishing Group, who first was excited about my manuscript and saw a potential to reach other widows who were going through the loss of their "beloved."

Thanks to Kim Stanford, my managing editor, who has guided me and helped me refine these pages to make them more presentable.

A special thanks to my family, who read my manuscript and encouraged and prayed for me during this process and who loved me and helped me through the "fog" of my grief. A special thanks to my son, David, who gave special attention to proofreading.

Thanks to Cathy Allen, Pat Westbrook and Pat and Charles Mason, who read my manuscript and gave valuable and insightful suggestions.

Thanks to Trent Hall for permission to use his wonderful poem, "What Is It About Heaven?"

Thanks for widow friends of mine, who prayed for me and inspired me in my "journey through the fog"—first, my beloved sister, Doris Swaringen, then my precious friends, Mary Buckner, Elizabeth Griffin, Mary Gustafson, Kathy Sorrell, Virginia Harrison, and Vonette Bright .

To God be the glory!

CONTENTS

THE RIGHTEOUS PASS AWAY; THE
GODLY OFTEN DIE BEFORE THEIR
TIME. AND NO ONE SEEMS TO
CARE OR WONDER WHY. NO ONE
SEEMS TO UNDERSTAND THAT
GOD IS PROTECTING THEM
FROM THE EVIL TO COME. FOR
THE GODLY WHO DIE WILL REST
IN PEACE. (ISAIAH 57:1 NLT)

PROLOGUE

This book is about a journey—a journey through the "fog" experienced by the new widow. I have been on this journey so I can assure you that the "fog" will lift. The piercing ache in your heart and the flood of tears will diminish.

I don't make this promise out of the store of my own strength, but out of trust in the eternal promise of God: "Weeping may endure for a night, but joy comes in the morning" (Psalm 30:5).

I want to share some timeless truths that have guided me through this darkest night of my soul. I want to encourage you to take time to reflect on the good memories and to take time to heal from this gaping wound. It will take time and Jesus.

Jesus is the healer of broken hearts. He is mending my heart as I depend upon Him. If you hand your broken heart over to Jesus, He will mend yours also.

Life is so mundane and so daily. I want to give you some practical pointers for dealing with the round of everyday life as you journey through the "fog."

I have been there. I have longed for Adrian's arms to be around me and to seek his counsel in difficult issues that have come since he passed away. I have said to myself, *If only I had someone to tell me what to do next!* I have cried out to God when I went to bed alone at night, "Help me, help me!" And He did.

I've been to the grocery store and wondered, *What do I buy now?* Before I always thought of what Adrian would want. I'm learning to say, "Thank you for the memories!"

I'm asking the question, "Who am I now that Adrian is gone?" I'm looking to Jesus for help today and hope for my tomorrows. I can assure you that He is more than sufficient to meet all your needs.

I've been to the grave, and I know he isn't there. I know that I should remember, but that I shouldn't linger. I'm learning to live by faith in a real world—a world in which things don't always turn out the way you wished.

I'm learning to take this journey one step at a time, leaning hard on Jesus. I'm learning to let Him fight my battles for me. Jesus is the Lord of hosts. He is my spiritual husband's name (see Isaiah 54:5).

I'm letting Him use my grief to identify with the sorrows of others and to point them through the "fog." Yes, the "fog" will lift as it has for me. But life isn't easy. It will always be lived depending on my Guide, the Lord Jesus Christ. He is my good Shepherd. I commend Him to you. If you hold on to His hand, He will lead you through the "fog."

FOREWORD

Adrian and I had just retired after fifty-four years as pastor and wife. We were looking forward to the retirement years—not to retire from ministry, but to allow a younger generation to take the lead.

My husband loved pastors, and he was looking forward to spending much of his retirement time training younger pastors, and I, to train their wives.

We loved to travel and planned to spend time with one another seeing different places as we continued to serve the Lord. We also wanted to spend more time with our children and grandchildren, and the new great grandchild who was on the way.

I had been a pastor's wife since I was eighteen years old. We were married in college and served a small country church one hundred fifty miles from our college. Then I became a mother and many years later a grandmother. That's all I have ever known and all I ever wanted to be.

Barely two months after Adrian's retirement the news came—colon cancer, which had spread to the liver. Everyone was shocked. But, we had faith in our great God and knew He was able to heal. We did all we knew to do, medically and nutritionally, and turned it over to God.

My husband was a remarkable man. He never complained. He kept going—traveling, preaching, and ministering to others.

About six months later he developed a cough, and I was concerned. The doctor sent him for an MRI. It was pneumonia. They sent him straight to the hospital.

When they put him on oxygen, I remember Adrian saying, "I'm so glad to be here." Our personal physician, Dr. "Mark," advised me to call our children to come to the hospital right away.

Our son, David, a missionary in Spain, immediately made the journey. Our oldest son, Steve, came from Florida; our daughter, Gayle, from Atlanta, Georgia; and our youngest daughter, Janice, came from Memphis, Tennessee. The next day they were joined by their families.

When Adrian went to the hospital, I never dreamed that he would die. Until the last I always knew God was able to heal him. But God didn't choose to do that.

We stood around Adrian's bed and quoted Scriptures, and he outlined them. We sang to him, told him how much we loved him, and prayed for him.

He had trouble breathing, and just couldn't make it any longer. I don't know if he heard me when I told him I would be all right—not to worry. He was always strong when I was weak, courageous when I was afraid. Now it was my turn!

Adrian, above all others, taught me to love the Word of God. When we were young we stood at the grave side of our baby Philip, and God was sufficient. I learned at that time to lean hard on Jesus and to dig deep into His marvelous Word.

I learned to praise God by faith, and one day that faith turned to feeling. I trusted God before, and I would trust Him now. God's Word was the basis for my life before. It would be my foundation now. No, I didn't feel like praising God, but I learned before that I could "faith" my praise to God.

Someone sent me a list of things you might experience when you lose a loved one. One of the items was that you might be bitter against God. I remember putting my finger on it and saying out loud, "I am not going to do that!" Why would I be so foolish? I would then have to climb over that bitterness to get to God. I needed Him too much to do that. Although my heart was breaking, I would choose by faith to trust Him.

I've always heard that difficulties can make you *better* or *bitter*. I've chosen to become *better*. God promised to help me: "Happy is he who has the God of Jacob for his help, whose hope is in the Lord his God" (Psalm 146:5).

Will you choose to join me in this journey of getting *better* day by day—of calling out to Him for help, and knowing that He will give you hope for your tomorrows?

I WILL REMEMBER

"I will remember the works of the LORD; surely I will remember Your wonders of old." (Psalm 77:11)

Adrian went to be with Jesus one week before Thanksgiving. It has been my custom for years to write down the things I'm thankful for during my quiet time on Thanksgiving morning. Why should that year be any different?

I still have that list of things, dated Thanksgiving, November 23, 2005. It begins with Jesus—my LORD and Savior—Who is always there. Then for His written Word—the Bible—which has fed me and given me strength, help, comfort, guidance, and hope.

Then follow memories about . . .

- Adrian, whom I have loved for more than sixty years and to whom I was married for fifty-four years.
- For sweet memories of our children, the five churches that we have served, trips we took, sorrows and joys we shared.

- For Adrian's love for me and his telling me every day that he loved me.
- For Adrian's wise leadership, his gratitude, his positive spirit, his wisdom, his love and knowledge of God's Word, his generosity, his courage to stand for truth and righteousness, and for his sense of humor.

Yes, I will remember all the blessings that God gave me through Adrian's life! Our home is filled with pictures and objects that remind me of him and the wonderful times we spent together. When our family gets together, we share memories about him. I've been writing them down so we can remember.

On the anniversary of his death, I wanted to do something to remember him, but not to be sad. I had an open house for family and friends. We told stories—some serious, some humorous. We laughed and we cried. He would have liked it. It was good to remember.

A precious lady, Mary Gustafson, whose husband was the president of the National Religious Broadcasters for many years, wrote me a letter. In it she shared about what the memories of her husband, Brandt, meant to her:

> "It's hard to believe that in just days (May 14) it will be six years since Brandt left for the celestial city. If I go by my 'feelings,' I would say it feels like a very short time ago.

Yet, as I look back, it is very evident that the Lord and His many angels have been walking this journey with me. He has given me a thankful heart for every year we did have. I am slowly learning that even death cannot rob me of the joy of all those many memories. How grateful I am that God created us with the capacity to remember. I pray that He makes mine sharper."

I couldn't have said it better than Mary. Yes, I will remember and continue to say, "Thank you," to my Lord for giving me many years to know, love, and share my life with my beloved Adrian.

I encourage you to remember.

THE PROFOUND
AND THE PRACTICAL

Life is made up of the *profound* and the *practical*. Of course, the *profound* forms the foundation of our lives.

This foundation is not built out of mortar and bricks, but from the Word of God. We must lean on Jesus, the living Word of God, knowing Him and bringing our grief and our needs to Him. We must learn to praise Him and give thanks to Him for all things.

To find intimacy with God is to build a strong foundation for all of life—for its joys and its sorrows. Of course, the *profound* is the most important part of our lives. If that foundation is missing, then the rest of life has nothing to rest upon and will be easily swept away when the storms of life come.

But, life is also made up of the *practical*. Oswald Chambers said that we must "work out what God has worked in." Indeed, God uses the practical, mundane things of life.

Your loved one's death could have come unexpectedly or at the end of an extended illness. You may still be in shock. No one is ever fully prepared for the day or the hour.

I remember thinking many days and even saying out loud, "If there was just someone who could tell me what to do next." Previously I had been good at multi-tasking. Now, one task at a time was sufficient.

Then I recalled what Jesus said, "Therefore do not worry about tomorrow . . . Sufficient for the day is its own trouble" (Matthew 6:34). So when life seems overwhelming, just "do the next thing."

He didn't mean we shouldn't plan for tomorrow, but that we shouldn't worry about tomorrow. I loved the motto I saw in my sister Doris's garden: "Don't worry about tomorrow. God is already there."

Until the "fog" lifts, don't try to think about what your future holds. Get out of bed, take a bath, get dressed, spend time alone with God, eat breakfast, clean up the house, walk the dog, pay the bills that are due—just do the next thing.

Of course, pray all during the day. I remember praying many times, "Lord, what should I do now?" He would show me the next thing. Then God reminded me one day that He had already given me a Counselor, His Holy Spirit. But I needed practical help many times. As I called out to Him to help me, I realized that God was sending people my way to help with practical things.

The *practical* touches every area of life, as does the *profound*. We must live with the two kept in balance.

If we spend the majority of our time studying the Bible and praying, but fail to exercise and eat nutritionally, we will be unhealthy.

The profound truth in God's Word, that my "body is the temple of the Holy Spirit" (1 Corinthians 6:19 NIV), must be worked out daily with wholesome food, proper exercise, and sleep. God will not overlook our neglect of these practical principles for our physical lives. They will impact not only the physical but also our spiritual lives.

So, a part of this book will encourage you to center your life on the Word of God—the living Word of God who is Jesus, and the written Word of God, which is the Bible.

The other part will focus on practical issues and how the Word can be believed, obeyed, and worked out daily in our practical lives.

THE
PROFOUND

THE LORD OF HOSTS
IS HIS NAME

The name of my earthly husband was Adrian.
I loved that name. It represented who he was to
me.

I still treasure the "love notes" that he dropped by
my desk in the sixth grade signed—Adrian. It was his
name that I joyfully took to be my own on our wedding
day on September 2, 1951—Mrs. Adrian Rogers. I was
always proud to be called by his name, because he was
a man of integrity and wisdom.

I now have another husband. Isaiah 54:5 declares
that because I am a widow, "Your Maker is your
husband, the LORD of hosts is His name."

I have loved the names of God for many years.
I've studied about them. I've claimed what they mean
as my very own. But I had never given much thought to
the name *Jehovah Sabaoth* (the Lord of hosts).

Yes, *Jehovah Sabaoth* is my present husband's name.
I began to notice other places in the Bible where that

name was mentioned. Adrian's name had meant to me love, courage, wisdom, integrity, and so many other things.

I wanted to study and learn what the name of my spiritual husband meant. I discovered that name throughout the Word of God and realized an even greater understanding of what it meant to me.

THE KING OF GLORY

His name means "the Lord of hosts." He is the leader of all the hosts of heaven. He fights my battles for me. Psalm 24:9–10 pictures Him, not only as the LORD of hosts, but as the King of glory.

> *Lift up your heads, O you gates, Lift up, you everlasting doors! And the King of glory shall come in.*
>
> *Who is this King of glory? The LORD of hosts, He is the King of glory. Selah.* (*Selah* means to pause and just think about that.)

MY REFUGE

One of my favorite psalms is Psalm 46. I memorized it years ago. When the 9/11 tragedy occurred in 2001, I decided to review this wonderful passage and to focus on its significant truths at this crucial time in our country. Later I realized that the president's wife, Laura Bush, had also made this psalm her focus.

Recently God led me to focus my heart on my spiritual husband's special name to me. I have been reminded of Psalm 46, verses 7 and 11. They are identical: "The LORD of hosts is with us; the God of Jacob is our refuge." What comfort I have found in this promise.

Adrian had been my earthly protector. If I heard something in the middle of the night, I would whisper, "Adrian, what's that noise?"

I remember a time when that happened. It sounded like someone was walking on our roof. He got up and walked to the front door where he could see out the glass at the roof over our bedroom. There he saw it—a raccoon holding on to the branch of a tree extending over the roof, jumping up and down.

We had a good laugh and went back to sleep. I would not have walked to the front door, but he did. Adrian was always a man of courage. I felt safe when he was there.

Although he is no longer here, if I hear a noise, I can call out to my Protector—my place of refuge—my Lord of hosts.

STRONG REDEEMER

Isaiah 54:5 says that God is my Redeemer. Jeremiah 50:34 declares that my Redeemer is strong.

> *Their Redeemer is strong; the* LORD *of hosts is His name. He will thoroughly plead their case, that He may give rest to the land.*

The Lord of hosts has come to set me free—to plead my cause, to give me rest. He will free me from my fears: fear of loneliness, fear of thieves or other predators, fear of lack of provision in any area—physical, emotional, or spiritual. And He longs to do that for you as well. He has done that for me as I have cried out to Him, "*Jehovah Sabaoth*, fight my battles for me."

I am reminded of the story of King Jehoshaphat, who was told that a great multitude was coming against him beyond the sea. He fasted and called on his God. This was his prayer: "O our God, will You not judge them? For we have no power against this great multitude that is coming against us; nor do we know what to do, but our eyes are upon You" (2 Chronicles 20:12).

I have experienced some tremendous problems since Adrian went to heaven. I have prayed this prayer many times, "O God, the multitudes are coming; I don't know what to do, but my eyes are on You." Whatever your battle, your spiritual husband, the LORD of hosts, will go before you. Do not be afraid!

One of my Adrian's favorite hymns was "A Mighty

Fortress." Previously, the name Lord *Sabaoth* had little meaning for me. Recently, when I was singing this magnificent song, I realized that there was His name in the second verse of this familiar song.

> Did we in our own strength confide,
> Our striving would be losing;
> Were not the right Man on our side,
> The Man of God's own choosing:
> Dost ask who that may be?
> Christ Jesus, it is He;
> Lord Sabaoth, His name,
> From age to age the same,
> And He must win the battle.
>
> —Martin Luther (1483–1546)

He will not just send His angelic hosts to fight my battles for me. He will lead the way into battle and will win the battle for me.

King Jehoshaphat was told to send the singers out first—that the battle was not theirs but God's. If only they would do their part, God would do His. Their part was to sing praises. They were to celebrate the victory even before it was won.

That is what we must also do—claim God's promises, but also sing His praises. Indeed He is able to fight the battle for us. He is not only a mighty general; He is the King—the King of glory. And this King of glory is my husband!

MY TWENTY-THIRD PSALM

The Lord is my Bridegroom and my Husband;
I shall not lack love and companionship.
He gives me understanding of His ways;
He understands all my needs and desires.
He longs to spend time to fellowship with me;
He leads me into quiet times with Him alone.
Yes, though I'm surrounded by
rejection and loneliness,
I will fear no evil; for You are with me.
I know that You love me, for I feel Your presence,
And I hear Your voice.
You loved me so much that You
laid down Your life for me;
You provide for every need I have;
You protect me from those who would do me harm.
Surely Your goodness and lovingkindness
Will be evident every day I live,
And I shall be united with my heavenly Bridegroom
And Husband forever.

–JR

(*Lean Hard on Jesus* by Joyce Rogers © 2005, pages 73–74. Used by permission of Crossway Books, a publishing ministry of Good News Publishers, Wheaton, IL 60187, www.crossway.org.)

THINK ABOUT HEAVEN

When Adrian went to heaven, I thought a lot about it. I read all the Scriptures about heaven. I sang all the songs I knew about heaven. I tried to visualize him there. I thought about all our loved ones and friends that he would meet in heaven and what a wonderful reunion that would be.

Heaven means different things to different people. Circumstances surrounding the death of each loved one cause us to visualize heaven in our own unique way. I found it helpful and I think it would be good for you to think about heaven too.

When my baby died suddenly, I made a conscious effort to give up to God my "so-called" right to understand why. He used a wonderful gospel song entitled "We'll Talk It Over" to help me do this. I visualized all of us one day sitting under a tree in heaven listening to Jesus tell us why.

Before my mother died she had Alzheimer's disease, so I rejoiced that in heaven she now knew all things.

My good friend, Virginia, suffered great pain before she died. I was so glad that in heaven, she would know no pain.

For the one who is crippled or disfigured, heaven means wholeness of body. To the blind, heaven means they can see. For the widow, nights are especially hard. What an encouragement to read in God's Word that there is no night in heaven. Instead, heaven is pictured as a place of beauty and perfection—gates of pearl and a street of pure gold.

For those of us who have experienced the loss of our loved ones, there have been many tears, heartaches, and sorrow. What a prospect to know that all our tears are wiped away and that heaven will be an end to our sorrows!

Yes, over and over, we are told wonderful truths about heaven in God's Word. A songwriter described heaven as a wonderful place filled with glory and grace. But God's Word is strangely silent about some things. What will we look like? What age will we be? What will we do in heaven?

We can't comprehend a timeless, ageless eternity. So we must be content with the knowledge that "when He is revealed, we shall be like Him, for we shall see Him as He is" (1 John 3:2). That is sufficient for me!

Someone has declared that we will all be thirty-three years old, because that's how old Jesus was when He died. That conclusion seems unfounded and somewhat absurd to me.

Some have said that it wouldn't be heaven if their dog or cat or horse weren't there. Others think it wouldn't be heaven if their loved one wasn't there. I certainly have my emotional preferences about heaven. Nevertheless, I am willing to turn all the uncertainties over to the Lord and rejoice in the knowledge that I shall see my Savior face-to-face, as stated below in a verse from "O That Will Be Glory":

O that will be glory for me,
Glory for me, glory for me,
When by His grace I shall look on His face,
That will be glory, be glory for me.

—Charles H. Gabriel (1856–1932)

A friend gave me this poem that he had written about heaven. His conclusion (as well as mine) is, of course, that heaven is all about wanting to see Jesus most of all!

WHAT IS IT ABOUT HEAVEN?

What is it about Heaven that makes
us want to go there?
Is it the golden streets, the gates of pearl,
the celestial air?
Why do we want to go to Heaven?
Is it the freshness, the freedom?
Is it the calmness of the sea
or the blessings there for me?
Is it freedom from disease,
and restoring of sight?
Or maybe no lack,
with blessings we partake.
Could it be that all these are just
"icing on the cake"?
For Jesus, the Bread of Life,
is making things just right.
To enjoy Him and He us—
and that's better by far
Than the blessings He gives,
for He is the Light.
He is the True One, the Lily, the Rose;
the Lion of Judah,
the Bright Morning Star.
Redeemer and Comforter,
our King and our Friend,

the Giver of life Who trusts in His Father
So we too can follow Him,
for there is no other
Who created us, sustains us,
forgives us, renews us,
Celebrates with us, sings over us,
invites us, involves us,
informs us, includes us,
crowns us, leads us, lives in us,
And blesses us.
No one else is worthy
of our ultimate devotion,
Or first place in our hearts;
the depth of His love
is beyond mere emotion.
For those who know Him,
He is the reason for Heaven,
For there we'll be home.

—Trent Hall, October 2, 2006, used by permission

"Let not your heart be troubled; you believe in God, believe also in Me. In my Father's house are many mansions; if it were not so, I would have told you. I go to prepare a place for you. And if I go and prepare a place for you, I will come again and receive you to Myself; that where I am, there you may be also. And where I go you know, and the way you know." Thomas said to Him, "Lord, we do not know where You are going, and how can we know the way?" Jesus said to him, "I am the Way, the truth, and the life. No one comes to the Father except through Me."
(John 14:1–6)

Then I, John, saw the holy city, New Jerusalem, coming down out of heaven from God, prepared as a bride adorned for her husband. And I heard a loud voice from heaven saying, "Behold, the tabernacle of God is with men, and He will dwell with them, and they shall be His people. God Himself shall be with them and be their God. And God will wipe away every tear from their eyes; there shall be no more death, nor sorrow, nor crying. There shall be no more pain, for the former things have passed away." (Revelation 21:2–4)

But I saw no temple in it, for the Lord God Almighty and the Lamb are its temple. The city had no need of the sun or of the moon to shine in it, for the glory of God illuminated it. The Lamb is its light. And the nations of those who are saved shall walk in its light, and the kings of the earth bring their glory and honor into it. Its gates shall not be shut at all by day (there shall be no night there). And they shall bring the glory and the honor of the nations into it. But there shall by no means enter it anything that defiles, or causes an abomination or a lie, but only those who are written in the Lamb's Book of Life.
(Revelation 21:22–27)

God's Word—My Greatest Resource

I am a lover of the Word of God. I believe every word is true.

So, when my husband left and went to heaven, I already knew what my greatest resource was for comfort and strength, direction and help. Of course, it was the Word of God.

This was not the first time I had experienced grief. When I was a young wife and mother, our third baby, little Philip, died by sudden "crib death."

At that time, I had leaned hard on Jesus, the living Word of God, and dug deep into His marvelous written Word. He had comforted me in my sorrow and I found Him to be sufficient. He pointed me to promises in His Word.

So many years later, when that one who was dearest to me—with whom I had shared my life for fifty-four years—left this world, I turned to the Word of God. I looked to promises that I knew from the past. Friends sent me verses, and I dug into the treasure of God's Word for a fresh message from Him. How precious all of these were to me.

It has been several years since my "beloved" took his heavenly flight. It has been a difficult time, but I am doing well. God has been faithful to sustain me. Yes, I've cried, I've been lonely, and sometimes longed for his counsel and for his loving arms to be around me.

But, from the store of His promises, I claimed Jesus to be my husband. I asked Him to put His arms around me and embrace me with His love—and He has.

For your Maker is your husband, the LORD of hosts is His name; and your Redeemer is the Holy One of Israel; He is called the God of the whole earth. (Isaiah 54:5)

In the time of grief, there is nothing else that can take the place of turning to the Living Word of God, the Lord Jesus, and the written Word of God, the Bible.

You must take time every morning to seek Him, asking for His guidance, protection, comfort, and strength.

If you find you are in need, cry out to Him for help. In those early days, and especially at night, I literally cried out to God, "Help me, help me!" And you know, He did. He wants to give help to you, just as He did for me.

I also read the promises that others sent me. I have so treasured three Bible verse collections. One was a small book of handwritten promises given to me by my precious friend, Marli, who lost her son several years ago by a freak accident. The other was a book of typewritten verses, a verse for every day of the month. It was sent to me by Brenda, a pastor's wife, whom I have never met. Yet I read them over and over, and what a blessing they were to me. Then my granddaughter, Rachel, typed out verses—one for every day in the month—and put them on small colorful squares of paper held together with a metal ring.

Some memorable passages were about *heaven*. I wanted to read those wonderful verses over and over. I visualized Adrian there with Jesus and other family members and friends, especially with our little Philip.

> *Let not your heart be troubled; you believe in God, believe also in Me. In my Father's house are many mansions; if it were not so, I would have told you. I go to prepare a place for you. And if I go and prepare a place for you, I will come again and receive you to Myself; that where I am, there you may be also. (John 14:1–3)*

Then, there were other verses about the resurrection and what it would be like. Yes, I sometimes go to his grave site. I even had my baby's body brought from Florida to be placed next to Adrian's body. I visualized what it will be like on that resurrection day when their bodies will be raised together and changed. What a day that will be when we are caught up together to meet Jesus in the skies!

> *Jesus said to her, "I am the resurrection and the life. He who believes in Me, though he may die, he shall live. And whoever lives and believes in Me shall never die. Do you believe this?" (John 11:25–26)*

I found promises about help for today.

> *For the Lord GOD will help Me; therefore I will not be disgraced; therefore I have set My face like a flint, and I know that I will not be ashamed. (Isaiah 50:7)*

I also found promises about hope for tomorrow.

> *This I recall to my mind, therefore I have hope. Through the LORD'S mercies we are not consumed, because His compassions fail not. They are new every morning; great is Your faithfulness. (Lamentations 3:21–23)*

Then there were promises about strength for my weaknesses.

> *The LORD God is my strength; He will make my feet like deer's feet. And He will make me walk on my high hills. (Habakkuk 3:19)*

There were words of comfort and assurance that my tears would be wiped away. Indeed, there were many tears.

> *O you afflicted one, tossed with tempest, and not comforted, behold, I will lay your stones with colorful gems, and lay your foundations with sapphires. I will make your pinnacles of rubies, your gates of crystal, and all your walls of precious stones. All your children shall be taught by the LORD, and great shall be the peace of your children. (Isaiah 54:11–13)*

How I treasure those promises that tell me that nothing separates me from God's love—not even death.

> *For I am persuaded that neither death nor life, nor angels nor principalities nor powers, nor things present nor things to come, nor height nor depth, nor any other created*

thing, shall be able to separate us from the love of God which is in Christ Jesus our Lord. (Romans 8:38–39)

Then there were verses to encourage me to pray, to call out to God.

Give ear to my prayer, O God, and do not hide Yourself from my supplication. Attend to me, and hear me; I am restless in my complaint, and moan noisily. (Psalm 55:1–2)

There are also verses to encourage me to sing praises to Him. I have done that every day. I love to sing to Him, and He loves to hear me sing. God is waiting for you to sing your solo just for Him.

O God, my heart is steadfast; I will sing and give praise, even with my glory. . . . I will praise You, O LORD, among the peoples, and I will sing praises to You among the nations. (Psalm 108:1, 3)

There are verses for when I am afraid.

The LORD is my light and my salvation; whom shall I fear? The LORD is the strength of my life; of whom shall I be afraid? (Psalm 27:1)

Verses of the assurance of the joy of the Lord.

Weeping may endure for a night, but joy comes in the morning. (Psalm 30:5)

Words to assure me of God's peace and care.

"Peace I leave with you, My peace I give to you; not as the world gives do I give to you. Let not your heart be troubled, neither let it be afraid." (John 14:27)

Verses to help me praise the Lord.

Because Your lovingkindness is better than life, my lips shall praise You. Thus I will bless You while I live; I will lift up my hands in Your name. (Psalm 63:3–4)

And then there is the assurance of everlasting life . . . I can be with Adrian forever. But, best of all, I can be with Jesus, who is eternal life.

> *"For God so loved the world that He gave His only begotten Son, that whosoever believes in Him should not perish but have everlasting life." (John 3:16)*

There is assurance of answered prayer.

> *"Call to Me, and I will answer you, and show you great and mighty things, which you do not know." (Jeremiah 33:3)*

There are verses to tell us to come to Him with a thankful heart.

> *Oh, give thanks to the LORD! Call upon His name; make known His deeds among the peoples! (Psalm 105:1)*

God's Word includes so many promises for you. Many of them are listed in Appendix A, "The Treasure of God's Word," beginning on page 79.

Read them over and over. Believe them. Obey them. Claim them as your very own.

VISUALIZE THE SCRIPTURES

The book of Psalms is my favorite book in the Bible. I have told others, "If you are hurting, just start reading in the book of Psalms, and God will meet you there."

The book of Psalms will bring comfort and strength. It will teach you how to pray, how to sing, and how to praise.

It is filled with symbolism. Use your sanctified imagination and visualize by faith the promises in God's Word. It will help heal your broken heart.

Let me give you several examples. A friend of mine, Carla McDowell, moved to Destin, Florida. One day I received a big brown envelope in the mail. It was filled with white feathers with this Scripture: "He shall cover you with His feathers, and under His wings you shall take refuge" (Psalm 91:4).

This was already one of my favorite Scriptures, but it helped me visualize God's shelter and protection for my life. I visualized myself running under His wings, where I would be safe.

I received an invitation to speak at a women's retreat. I accepted largely because their theme was "Under the Shadow of His Wings," and that's where I had been living. In preparation for that day, I studied all the references about being "under His wings." Perhaps these precious thoughts He gave me will bless you as they did me.

- We will all experience storms in our lives.
- The solution is the same, no matter what the storm. You must run—run as fast as you can under the shadow of His wings.
- How do you get under the shadow of His wings? It's by *trusting*—trusting God. Psalm 91:4 says, "under His wings you shall take refuge."
- How do you trust Him? You have to get to know Him through His Word and through prayer—spending time with Him.
- What do you find when you get under His wings? You find Him—the Father, the Son, the Holy Spirit. He is able to meet every need you have.

He is your **protector**.
He is your **lover**.
He is your **song**.
He is your **lovingkindness**.
He is your **help** and your **hope**
And **everything** you need!

Another verse I love is Psalm 18:29, "For by You I can run against a troop, by my God can I leap over a wall."

I have visualized myself many times holding on to Jesus' hand and running through that enemy in my life, and leaping over that wall (that problem or obstacle).

Then there is Psalm 18:16, "He sent from above, He took me; He drew me out of many waters."

I have pictured myself drowning in my grief or problem. Then Jesus reaches down, holds on to me, soaked and shivering, and pulls me to the safety of His arms.

Psalm 23 is filled with spiritual imagery. Oh, I see my Good Shepherd leading me through that fearsome, dark valley of the shadow of death. Yet, He protects me with His rod and staff and brings me through. Oh, praise His Holy Name! I don't have to walk through that valley alone.

My friend, Kathy, who is also a widow, told me how she pondered the life of Jochebed, Moses' mother. She was impressed that it took great faith for Jochebed to save her baby's life by putting him in a basket and pushing him out into the reeds of the Nile River.

Kathy realized that God was telling her to trust Him with her situation, just like Jochebed did. He wanted her to take her circumstances and push them out into the river of God's love and protection, and trust Him to take care of every detail. Just as Jochebed trusted God, so we should trust Him.

You try it now. How about starting with Psalm 61:2–4:

From the end of the earth I will cry to You, when my heart is overwhelmed; lead me to the rock that is higher than I. For You have been a shelter for me, a strong tower from the enemy. I will abide in Your tabernacle forever; I will trust in the shelter of Your wings.

Or Psalm 107:28–30:

Then they cry out to the LORD in their trouble, and He brings them out of their distresses. He calms the storm, so that its waves are still. Then are they glad because they are quiet; so He guides them to their desired haven.

CALM THE STORM

Oh, Lord if You rule
The raging of the sea,
You can calm this tempest
Deep inside of me.
The waves rise up like
Billows in my soul;
You still them so that
My spirit is made whole.
In the storms of life
I cry to You, my God,
"Calm the storm,
Still the waves;
Take me from
The waters."
Then I'm glad because
The storm is quiet;
You gently comfort, guide,
And lead me safely home.

–JR

(Taken from Psalms 18:16; 89:9; 107:25–30)
(*Lean Hard on Jesus* by Joyce Rogers © 2005, page 140. Used by
permission of Crossway Books, a publishing ministry of Good News
Publishing, Wheaton, IL 60187, www.crossway.org.)

PACING YOURSELF

Life goes on—day by day. Before I get up in the morning I "pace" myself spiritually. This is something that Adrian taught me to do. It's contained in an acrostic.* I pray these words to the Lord. Why not begin your day using this helpful method to "pace" yourself.

PRAISE—"I praise You, Lord, that You gave Yourself *for* me."

ACCEPTANCE—"I accept that You gave Yourself *to* me."

CONTROL—"I place myself *under* Your control."

EXPECTATION—"I'm expecting it to be a great day."

*Taken from *What Every Pastor Ought to Know Workbook* by Adrian and Steve Rogers and the Pastor Training Institute (2006), 84.

PILLOW YOUR SOUL ON THE PROMISES OF GOD

My special friend, Carla, gave me a pillowcase with the following ten Old Testament names of God embroidered on it. She did not tell me what to do with the pillowcase or what the names meant; she just knew of my great love for God's names.

These names have special meanings and were revealed at different occasions in the Old Testament. I found it helpful. I would like to suggest that you read each Scripture listed and then study their background as to what they meant in Old Testament times.

Jehovah	—	Lord (Isaiah 26:4)
Jireh	—	Provider (Genesis 22:8, 14)
Shalom	—	Peace (Judges 6:23–24)
Shammah	—	He is there (Ezekiel 48:35)
Sabaoth	—	Lord of Hosts (Isaiah 54:5)
Nissi	—	Victory or Banner (Exodus 17:15)
Rohi	—	Shepherd (Psalm 23:1)

Rapha   —   Healer (Hosea 6:1)
Tsidkenu   —   Righteousness (Jeremiah 23:6)
M'Kaddesh —   Sanctifier (Leviticus 20:7–8)

The LORD who was real to Abraham, and others, will be just as real to you today in your special hour of sorrow and need.

He will be *your* Shepherd
He will be *your* Provider
He will be *your* Healer
He will be *your* Peace
He will be *your* Victory
And everything else you need.

Remember that He is always there. He has promised to "never leave you nor forsake you" (Hebrews 13:5).

To know His names and what they mean is a great avenue to knowing God more intimately. You will find that it is an exciting adventure to search for and know His names. There is a special blessing in God's Word for those who honor God and meditate on His names.

Malachi 3:16 says that if you do these things your name will be written down in God's special Book of Remembrance: "So a book of remembrance was written before Him for those who fear the LORD and who meditate on His name."

Oh, how I love His names; they are precious to me.

When I received my pillowcase, I began a new tradition. Each night before bed as I kneel down to pray, I lay my hand over each name and call it out to God. I claim what that name means for my life. And then I thank Him for all He means to me.

For instance, "You are *Jehovah*—my Lord. You are *Jehovah Jireh,* my Provider. Thank you for providing for all my needs today."

Then I gleaned from a book entitled *The Names of God* by Elmer Towns that all of these names were represented in Psalm 23. This psalm has been a favorite of mine since I memorized it when I was a child. Let me illustrate.

> The LORD *(Jehovah—my Lord)*
> Is my shepherd *(Rohi—my Shepherd)*
> I shall not want *(Jireh—my Provider)*
> He makes me to lie down in green pastures
>   *(Jireh—my Provider)*
> He leads me beside the still waters
>   *(Shalom—my Peace)*
> He restores my soul *(Rapha—my Healer)*
> He leads me in the paths of righteousness
>   *(Tsidkenu—my Righteousness)*
>   for His name's sake
> Yea, though I walk through the Valley of the
>   Shadow of Death I will fear no evil

For You are with me *(Shammah—*
always there with me)
Your rod and Your staff, they comfort me
(Rapha—my Healer)
You prepare a table before me *(Jireh—my*
Provider)
in the presence of my enemies *(Nissi—*
my Victor; Sabaoth—Lord of Hosts)
You anoint my head with oil
my cup runs over
(M'Kaddesh—my Sanctifier)
Surely goodness and mercy shall follow me
All the days of my life *(Jireh—my*
Provider)
And I will dwell in the house of the LORD
forever *(Shammah—always there with*
me)

I personalize this psalm. For instance, "Lord, you are my shepherd . . ." Then I ask Him to be all I need, and thank Him by faith that He will be all I need. Oh, what a wonderful Lord!

I recall what my pastor-husband would say at the close of the Lord's Supper at our church. He would open the Bible and share a promise from God's Word. Then, he would say:

"Go home and lay your head upon your
    pillow
And pillow your soul on the Word of God
And go to sleep and sleep well
For He Who watches Israel shall neither
    slumber nor sleep."

I do this every night and I sleep well, for I am confident that He is *Jehovah Shammah*—my Lord who is always there.

This is not something magical—a ritual to perform. Only if you mean what you pray and truly claim by faith who God is to you, represented in His names, will He bring sweet peace, comfort, and all you need.

Of course, you don't have to have a pillowcase with the names of God. Study and claim what these names of God mean to you. At the end of this book, you will find further comments written by my husband, Adrian, on some of my favorite names of God.

Although these are Old Testament names for God, all of these names are culminated in the New Testament in "the name which is above every name . . . Jesus" (Philippians 2:9–10).

The angel of the Lord appeared to the virgin Mary and said, "You shall call His name Jesus, for He will save His people from their sins" (Matthew 1:21). The name *Jesus* means "Jehovah saves."

We are told in the New Testament "that at the name of Jesus every knee should bow and that every tongue should confess that Jesus Christ is Lord to the glory of God the Father" (Philippians 2:10–11).

Romans 10:9 says, "If you will confess with your mouth the Lord Jesus and believe in your heart that God has raised Him from the dead, you will be saved." Romans 10:13 says, "For whoever calls on the name of the Lord shall be saved."

If you have not called upon His name, invite Jesus to be the Lord of your life and do it now. Only then will you know Him personally through His other names.

*"Kings and kingdoms will all pass away,
but there's something about that name."*

—William and Gloria Gaither

THE PRACTICAL

ONE OR THE OTHER MUST STAY

For those of us who have "lost" a mate, it seems like a destructive tornado has swept away our home and left another next to it unharmed. There is no rhyme or reason why one is taken and the other left. Someone spoke to this "fact of life."

One or the other must leave,
One or the other must stay.
One or the other must grieve,
That is forever the way.
That is the vow that was sworn,
Faithful 'til death do us part.
Braving what had to be borne,
Hiding the ache in the heart.
One, howsoever adored,
First must be summoned away.
That is the will of the Lord
One or the other must stay.

—Anonymous

You and I are the ones who are left. Try as we may to understand, we will not. That's just the way it is, and we must go on.

We must seek to find out what purpose God has for us now. How will we make it when that one who was closer to us than anyone on earth is gone? I remember saying to my husband before he died, "I'll be OK." I don't know if he heard me, and I didn't exactly know what that meant. I just knew from the depths of my soul that God would take care of me. And, indeed He has!

I wouldn't say it has been easy, but God brought me through that incredibly difficult first year, and I still know that He will be here for me.

A Practical "To-Do" List

After the funeral is over and loved ones have gone home, you are faced with the mundane decisions of what to do. What should I do first on the long "to-do" list (i.e., thank-you notes, financial decisions, and so on)?

Someone gave me a booklet that listed these possibilities. It didn't contain everything I needed to remember, but it was such a help. Listed below is a list of some of these tasks that I found helpful.

Thank-You Notes

The funeral home should supply note cards. Others may help, but it is a good idea for you to write some of them yourself.

- Send to family and friends who pitched in to help. Make your own list of these and prioritize which to write first.

- Send to family and friends who sent flowers and memorials.
- Send to those who brought food.

FINANCIAL DECISIONS

Financial decisions will vary according to your particular circumstances. I was the one in our family who wrote the checks, so I knew where the financial records were and how to manage it. This doesn't mean that I didn't need a reminder. There were times that I let the due date on a bill pass simply because I was still living in a "fog."

It may sound so simple, but pay your monthly bills and check your statement. I do online banking, and I still forget to check my statement sometimes.

Have various financial papers transferred to your name. Send death certificates to the appropriate institutions. The funeral home will send you several copies of the death certificate. You can get more if you need them. They typically arrive about a month after the death of your mate. The death certificate gives verification of all the details of your mate's death.

If you have a financial advisor, he will help you have accounts listed in your name. If you have no advisor, you should enlist the advice of a knowledgeable person who has only your best interests at heart. Here are a few of the accounts you need to include:

- House (if you own one and it was listed in both of your names).
- Insurance
- Investments
- Bank account (if it was a joint account). I was advised not to do this right away in case a check came in with my husband's name on it.
- Phone bill (suggested but not mandatory).
- Utilities (suggested but not mandatory).
- Call your local Social Security office. Do this as soon as you can. If both you and your spouse received benefits, you will continue to receive benefits, but one of the benefits will stop. You will receive the larger amount.

A letter should be written to notify any person or organization of your mate's death. This involves a request to transfer any official document or listing solely to your name that may have been in your husband's name or been in both of your names.

- Credit card companies—Visa, American Express, Master Card, etc.
- Your church (for the church records)
- The Internal Revenue Service. If you have someone to help you already, they will know what to do so that you can file the appropriate returns.

MAKE A BUDGET

Begin to make a budget that is now just for one person. This may be difficult at first. Some expenses may remain the same, but some will change (such as food, gasoline, clothes, toiletries).

My financial advisor asked me to submit a budget with projected expenses. For a year I kept a detailed record of all my expenditures, and then I made a new budget that was just for one.

My financial advisor gives me wise advice, since he knows my financial state and can help project what my average budget for the year should be. My husband and I were past retirement age, so he knows how much I will need to meet my living expenses. He also assists in investment advice so I can continue earning income.

If you and your husband did not have such an advisor, I encourage you to seek someone whom you trust to help and advise you.

MAINTAIN A BALANCED LIFE

For quite a while these mundane duties may well consume a good part of your time. But allow time for other things such as moments alone with God, exercise, relaxation, and fellowship with friends and family.

Endeavor to maintain a balanced life. Do the tasks that are "have tos" but don't feel like you have to do all these things on the to-do list right away. Ask your Chief Counselor to show you what needs to be done today. Of course, He is the Holy Spirit. He has promised to guide you and He will.

If you find yourself overwhelmed, stop and take a break—go to God in prayer, relax, visit with family and friends, or just take the dog for a walk.

DIFFERENT CIRCUMSTANCES

Every widow will have things in common, but every person also has different circumstances.

We become widows at different ages, have different financial circumstances, different families, etc. Some with careers must go back to work soon after the death of their loved one. For some that is good, but for others it may be overwhelming. Others are older in retirement and may not be in good health.

But, whatever our circumstances, we must discover who we are now that our mate is gone.

I married my childhood sweetheart, and we were married for fifty-four wonderful years. I was a full-time homemaker and pastor's wife. I worked full time, but it was at home and doing volunteer work.

When Adrian retired, we had many plans for our retirement years. Who am I now? What will I do?

These could be overwhelming questions, but I have taken one day at a time. Some things I've continued to do (such as sing in the choir). I have spoken to some ladies' groups in the past. So now it seems natural to accept a few speaking engagements. I have shared lessons that I have learned along the way.

I have done some writing in the past. I have a penchant for writing down "reflections" on experiences and what God has taught me. During this last year, I have written down a few things but was never greatly moved to sit down and write until recently. Before now, I felt like God was teaching me, guiding me, helping me through each day.

Now that my "fog" has lifted, I find myself reaching out to other widows and wanting to share some of the lessons God has taught me.

I have only been on this new journey a short time. I've learned so much, but there is so much more to understand. *Lord, I'm listening—help me be obedient to what I have learned.*

DON'T MAKE SUDDEN CHANGES

I have heard this advice a number of times, "Don't make major changes or decisions at least for a year." This is good advice. However, depending on the circumstances, you may have no choice.

- Don't sell your house and move unless you have to. The familiar surroundings will help you adjust. But, if you have to because of financial or health reasons, then seek counsel and trust God. He will see you through.

- Don't make major purchases unless you have to. Don't be swept away by some con artist who would take advantage of a widow with some promise of great dividends for a risky investment.
- Don't get involved romantically before your heart has healed. Learn to lean on your "spiritual husband," the Lord of Hosts, and allow Him to meet your needs spiritually, emotionally, and physically before you even begin to think of someone else.

Many of you will remain unmarried the rest of your life. Plan to be content with this prospect. Trust God with your future. Allow God to be in control.

I know godly friends for whom God brought another love into their lives, and they are very happy. I know others who jumped into another relationship too quickly and it brought great unhappiness.

Healthy Habits

Good Nutrition

Since I was already a believer in and advocate for healthy eating, it was not as difficult for me to practice good eating habits when my husband died.

This was already my way of living. I was committed to a healthy lifestyle. But I did have to *continue* to practice that which I believed.

It would have been easy to slack off. It is harder to cook for one and certainly isn't fun eating alone. Yet, I made a conscious effort to continue eating nutritiously.

Let me encourage you to either continue or to begin eating in a healthy way. It is an adjustment, cooking for just one. But it will be well worth the effort in regard to how you feel. Let me give you some hints on healthy eating for one. Simple, healthy meals can be easy to fix.

Hints for Healthy Eating for One

- I make my own whole wheat bread and grind my own whole grain flour. I have a bread making machine. I make just one loaf at a time. When it cools, I cut it and slip two slices into each zip-lock bag, and put them in the freezer. That way it is easy to defrost.

- I can quickly make a healthy sandwich—a tuna fish salad sandwich, or a peanut butter and banana, honey and cinnamon open-faced sandwich. A favorite of mine is an open-faced sandwich with sliced avocados laid on sliced tomatoes with grated cheese and toasted in my toaster oven.

- Stir-fry fresh vegetables with pieces of chicken over brown rice. This is easy to make for one. I make vegetable or bean soup and put the leftovers in small containers in the freezer.

- Omelets are easy to fix. I frequently sauté green onions and asparagus or spinach and tomatoes, and sprinkle with a little cheese. I may put a small potato in the microwave and top it with a little butter or yogurt. I eat that with a piece of whole wheat toast—that's delicious!

- Sometimes I make vegetable spaghetti with soy meat and serve it over whole wheat spaghetti along with a tossed salad.

- I fix lots of fresh salads with a variety of good

vegetables. I prepare slaw mixed with chopped apples or pineapple bits and raisins mixed with a little mayonnaise and yogurt.

- Grated carrot salad is good also. A favorite of mine is a mixture of greens (romaine and red leaf spinach) with sliced strawberries, purple onion rings, and chopped walnuts, mixed with raspberry vinaigrette.

- Occasionally I make a pot of chicken vegetable stew and, of course, save the leftovers in containers for the freezer.

- I love salmon, so I try to fix it often—broiled or canned—made into a salmon patty or salmon salad sandwich on some homemade whole wheat bread.

Breakfast Ideas

- I am an avid breakfast eater. My basic breakfast would be hot oatmeal served with blueberries or bananas, topped with plain yogurt, honey, and chopped walnuts. Sometimes I fix fresh muesli with oatmeal, yogurt, with fruit and walnut pieces.

- Sometimes I scramble an egg or fix an omelet and have a piece of whole wheat toast and a piece of fruit—such as an orange or grapefruit half. Occasionally I fix some soy meat sausage.

- My husband loved whole wheat/oatmeal pancakes. Sometimes I fix these pancakes topped with blueberries or bananas or strawberries and yogurt, with chopped nuts and real maple syrup. Sometimes I put the batter in the waffle iron and make some delicious waffles. Of course I freeze the leftovers to eat later.

- I always fix pancakes when my grandchildren spend the night.
- Another easy breakfast or lunch is to spread a piece of whole wheat toast with peanut or almond butter and mash half a banana over it and drizzle it with honey. (Just make sure it's natural nut butter, not hydrogenated.)

Lunch or Supper Ideas

- For a special lunch with friends, I fix a fresh pineapple "boat" filled with pineapple chunks, sliced bananas, grapes, blueberries, and nuts (coconut is optional). Steamed chopped chicken breast can be added with a touch of curry. Mix with mayonnaise and yogurt. Serve with whole wheat blueberry or banana nut muffins and it's gourmet. You may leave out the chicken and serve plain or topped with plain yogurt and sprinkled with coconut.
- Fix a pot of vegetable soup or bean soup and serve with corn bread or whole wheat toast.
- A favorite company dinner is Cornish hens served

with brown rice mixed with mandarin oranges and sliced almonds with sautéed asparagus. For the salad, try mixed greens with sliced strawberries, red onion slices, and walnuts and served with raspberry vinaigrette.

• You can even fix a small healthy pizza out of a whole wheat tortilla. Spread with tomato sauce, vegetables (broccoli, green onions, zucchini, mushrooms) and sprinkle with cheese and toast in your toaster oven.

• You can also fix a sandwich "wrap," using whole wheat tortillas and adding vegetables, tuna, salmon, or chicken.

• There's a variety of ways to fix a fruit salad, topped with either yogurt or cottage cheese.

• There's a quickie lunch fixed by stuffing a tomato with cottage cheese, tuna or chicken salad on romaine lettuce. Serve with a piece of whole wheat toast.

Desserts

I don't eat sugary desserts as a rule; I make an exception occasionally. I do make healthy oatmeal cookies and muffins made with whole wheat flour and store the leftovers in my freezer. One or two of them with a cup of hot tea satisfies me.

I always keep a basket of fruit—according to what is in season—oranges and grapefruit, grapes and kiwi, bananas and apples. Then I always keep blueberries and other berries in the refrigerator.

Sweeteners

I am an advocate for raw, natural local honey. You still can't eat much, however, if you wish to maintain a healthy diet.

Sucanat (found in health food stores) is a natural form of cane sugar that I use to bake with—usually mixed with some honey. It is more expensive, but I don't use that much, so it doesn't matter.

I hope I have inspired you on your way to healthy eating. It will make a big difference in how you feel. It's your choice!

I have written a book on nutrition. If you are interested, it is entitled *The Bible's Seven Secrets for Healthy Eating.*

Suggestions

Here are some tips that I hope you will find helpful.

- Invest in a bread machine. Eventually buy a grain mill and grind your own whole grain flour. If I can't convince you to do that, buy the healthiest whole wheat bread you can find with *no* hydrogenated shortening.
- Invest in a juicing machine.

Nutritional no's:
1. White flour
2. White sugar
3. White rice
4. Hydrogenated shortening, margarine, lard, and animal fat
5. Drinks with caffeine and aspartame
6. Pork products—pork chops, bacon, sausage, ham

Nutritional yes's
1. At least five to seven servings of fresh vegetables and fruit each day
2. Whole wheat or whole grain bread
3. Oatmeal and brown rice
4. Eight eight-ounce glasses of water per day
5. Olive oil
6. Raw, local honey

SLEEP

Get at least eight hours of sleep. Kneel before the Lord before you go to bed. Turn your cares, heartaches, and fears over to Him. Ask Him to give His "beloved" sleep. Remember: You are His beloved, and He neither slumbers nor sleeps (see Psalm 121:4).

I will both lie down in peace, and sleep: for You alone, O LORD, make me dwell in safety. (Psalm 4:8)

EXERCISE

Walk every day if you can. I walk two to three miles most days. My dog, Akie, comes along with me, and his health is benefited also. I also lift weights and do strength exercises several times each week. These habits make me feel so much better.

A POSITIVE ATTITUDE

A positive attitude with a good sense of humor is extremely healthy. Remember, the Bible says, "A merry heart does good, like medicine" (Proverbs 17:22).

Faith will produce a positive attitude, so start there. If you become negative, stop and check first your spiritual habits of prayer and study of God's Word. Then check on your physical habits of good nutrition, exercise, and sleep.

THE IMPORTANCE
OF FRIENDS

I cannot emphasize enough the importance of
friends at this time—especially those who will call and
encourage you. You need a friend with whom to go to
lunch or supper, someone with whom you can pour
out your heart. Then you need a friend with whom you
can have fun and laugh.

My lifelong friend, Barbara, is such an encourager.
I'm sorry that she lives so far away, but we can still stay
in touch by phone. She has been a widow for many
years. Here are her words of advice:

> My husband died after a long, long
> illness. God measured out His grace day
> by day and enabled me to work and take
> care of him at night. Just when I thought
> I could not hold on physically, God called
> him home. Because of his long illness,
> early retirement and the need for me to

work to supplement our income, I had lost contact with everyone.

The thing that He has done for me that enriched my life during my husband's illness and the last fourteen years, are the people He has brought along my path. He brought so many ladies I knew from my younger days—not all at once, but one at a time. Joyce sent me a CD entitled *In Time of Trouble*. And it arrived on the day I needed it the most. I know that God provided these ladies just when I needed them and He still does today.

My advice to women living alone is to reconnect with your friends of long ago and try to make some new ones. Laugh a lot and be thankful for what you have. Make your telephone your friend and use it often. Also, the computer is a wonderful way to connect every day with friends and the information network.

It should not only be a friend with whom you can pour out your heart, but a friend who can share her heart with you also. It needs to be a mutual friendship. Also, as you share your needs, pray together.

My friend, Pat, is such a wonderful person. We have

a unique friendship because we share two wonderful grandsons who live far across the ocean. This is because their parents—my son, David, and her daughter, Kelly, are missionaries to Spain. We don't get to see them often, but we pray for them.

Pat lives two hours away, but we talk often on the phone. She often prays for me and I for her before we hang up.

Then there is JoAnn, who came to the hospital when Adrian was so ill and took me out to lunch and just let me talk. She calls often just to ask how I am. Sometimes we go to lunch and talk and talk.

Kathy is also a widow. Sometimes we go to church together or out to eat. We talk about serious things or we laugh together. We pray together and encourage one another.

Wanda is my neighbor. She calls to check on me or we'll stop to chat when I take my dog for a walk. We share each other's burdens. Her two daughters, Susan and Sandy, have died in the past couple years, so there have been moments when it was time for me to reach out to her and her husband, Robert.

Elizabeth is a new widow. I've known her for years, but we didn't get to spend a lot of time together. But since her husband died and I'm alone, we've gone out to eat a number of times. She's like a member of the family. She and her husband, Neil, used to babysit two of my granddaughters who are now grown. One day I called and asked her if she wanted to come to my grandson, Andrew's, basketball game. She came and enjoyed it and we enjoyed having her there.

Yes, friends are a gift from God. Appreciate and cherish them!

MY DOG, AKIE

My children decided that I needed a dog and they wanted to get me a puppy for Christmas (Adrian had died November 15). We researched different kinds of dogs and they took me to see puppies. But I finally decided that I didn't need the responsibility of training a puppy so soon after Adrian died, so I didn't get a dog for Christmas.

Several months later a family from our church, who raised Maltese puppies, wanted to give me their last puppy. The two teenagers had named him Adrian Pierce, after my husband. They called him A. P.

God had laid it on their hearts to give me this darling snow-white puppy. They brought him over for me to see. He came complete with puppy food, vitamins, dog pocketbook carrier, bed, and blue satin baby blanket. I couldn't resist, so I kept him.

At the time I couldn't bring myself to call him A. P., so I named him Akie, my husband's nickname when he was a little boy.

Little Akie is truly a gift from God. Frequently I say, "Thank You, God, for my little doggie." It's so nice to have a friendly and excited doggie to which I can come home. And talk about being spoiled!

When my children were growing up, we had a wonderful dog named Tawny, a Weimaraner. She was a house dog but was never allowed on the furniture, and certainly not in our bed. We had her for eleven years and thought that there would never be another dog like Tawny, who had totally won my heart.

The first time I saw Akie sitting in my husband's chair, I said, "Get down!" But by and by I thought, *Why does it really matter? The dog doesn't shed and I keep him clean.* So this dog is not only allowed on the furniture, but he sleeps with me in my bed. Yes, "Thank You, Lord, for Akie."

HE WANTS TO USE YOU!

You may not feel like getting back to doing what you were used to doing. However, let me encourage you to get back into a routine.

I went back to church right away. Even if I cried, I knew that's where God wanted me.

After several weeks I decided that it was time to resume teaching the children's new member class, which I had taught for more than thirty years. It was so good for me to be used by God, even when I was hurting.

Then soon after, I started back singing in the choir. This had been a large part of my life. And, indeed, music helps heal the broken heart.

It was just one step at a time.

One Step at a Time

Only a step
One step at a time
Don't let me walk
Ahead of you
Nor linger far behind;
I look out far ahead
And cannot see
Just one step with You,
Dear Lord
Is quite enough for me.

—JR

(*Becoming A Women of Wisdom* by Joyce Rogers © 2001, page 27.
Used by permission of Crossway Books, a publishing ministry of
Good News Publishing, Wheaton, IL 60187, www.crossway.org.)

I was still processing my grief when I heard of two other women, whom I knew, whose husbands had joined Adrian in Glory. I called them and prayed for them. I began a prayer list of widows.

Since Adrian's death, I now have a list of women whose husbands have died. I have tried in various ways to reach out to them. I have walked where they are walking.

My "fog" has lifted. I am not quite sure when it happened, but about six or eight months later I realized it was gone. I recently assured a new widow that her "fog" would one day lift and things would be better if she kept "leaning hard" on Jesus.

For months I was occupied with opening sympathy cards, writing thank-you notes, and speaking on the phone to those who called to express their love. Friends called to invite me to lunch and dinner. These expressions of love helped in the healing process.

One day I realized I had passed another milestone. I called to invite a new widow to lunch with me and listen to her concerns and assure her of God's love and comfort.

Several invitations came for me to speak to various groups. I accepted and began to share how God was working in my life. Yes, God used other people in my life. Now He wanted to use me to bring comfort to others.

Valentine's Day is a "bummer" for widows. My first Valentine's Day after Adrian died was hard. My youngest daughter, Janice, and her husband, Bryan, took me to a lovely dinner, and that really helped. On my second Valentine's Day alone, Janice and Bryan took me to a special dinner again. But I ventured out a little and asked my precious friend, Elizabeth, out to a Valentine lunch that day. Her husband had been gone just a week. I even purchased a Valentine at the drugstore for her. Until then it had been too painful to even walk down that aisle.

When I went through my third Valentine's Day without Adrian, I began to think that it was time to do a little more for someone else. The Lord put on my heart the idea to have a nice Valentine's luncheon for some widows that I knew personally. I invited thirteen ladies. I got out my good china, crystal, and silver and set a beautiful table. My daughter, Janice, my daughter-in-law, Kelly, and Beth helped me. We served soup, little sandwiches, frozen fruit salad, and little muffins and cookies with hot tea.

After lunch we went into the living room and I shared how God had ministered to my life through His wonderful Word. Then I asked them all to share about their sweethearts. It was such a sweet time. They all said that they enjoyed it so very much. But the person who enjoyed it most of all was me. As I reached out to others, God reached back to me. Let me encourage you to reach out to others in their grief and problems. God doesn't want us to waste our sorrows.

I encourage you to be used by God. Take the sorrow that God has entrusted to you and be faithful with it. Look to Jesus! Trust Him! Learn from Him! And then reach out to your hurting world—not just to others who have lost their mates, but to whatever hurting soul God brings your way.

A GRATEFUL SPIRIT

My sister, Doris, has been a widow for more than twenty-two years. She is one of the most contented, joyful people I know. She doesn't have an abundance of material provisions, but she is content with what she has.

She loves to spend time with her "spiritual husband, Jesus." She rejoices in Him every day. She loves to spend time in her yard, working with her hands, planting flowers, and weeding. She has told me of lessons that God teaches her in her garden.

Doris prays for and encourages her children and grandchildren. She attends baseball games in which her grandson plays. She goes on long walks to keep herself fit. She is a prayer warrior not only for her family, but for mine. I do not know a more grateful or satisfied Christian than my sister. She inspires me in my journey with my "spiritual husband," Jesus.

I know other widows who have such a grateful spirit. Elizabeth had been a widow for only one week on the occurrence of her fifty-third wedding anniversary. I called to tell her I was thinking about her at this "tender time."

She expressed such gratitude for all God had done for her. She said to me, "How can I say thanks again?" She was grateful that her husband didn't have to linger any longer in his suffering.

Then there's Mary, my friend who has been a widow for many years. She teaches children and helps in a widows' share group. She's always filled with joy. Leona, whose husband has been gone for a few years, wrote a book for children entitled *The Orphan Lamb*. It's been translated into more than twenty languages and has been sent around the world.

Then there's my friend, Martha. Her husband, Ben, died in the Bahamas, when we were on a cruise. I was with her in the hospital when Ben had surgery and didn't make it. She had such a grateful spirit. She said thank you to every person who was endeavoring to help. She even expressed her gratitude to the Bahamian surgeon who came to tell her that Ben had died of a heart attack on the operating table. Her spirit of gratitude deeply impacted my life.

God uses these widows in a remarkable way that they would have never imagined. My friend Margot has a special love for Israel and enlisted in their "special army of volunteers" for a few weeks. She worked in their kitchen helping cook and bake. This may be out of your comfort zone, but somewhere God has a place and plan for you.

JUST THE BEGINNING OF YOUR JOURNEY

This is just the beginning of your journey. I wanted to help you through the "fog" that exists during the early months of being a widow.

I wanted to introduce you to my guide, the Lord Jesus Christ. He knows the way. In fact, He is the Way. If you will lean hard upon Him, He will see you through. His written Word, the Bible, has been my guidebook. It has brought encouragement and strength, help and hope. This treasure of promises awaits you. Dig deep into His marvelous Word.

I have made it through the "fog"—the fog of tears and disappointment, the fog of loneliness and confusion. You can make it too if you will daily depend on Jesus.

Then continue on. He has a plan for your life. He wants to use you and, yes, even your grief to bring hope to others who have also begun this journey.

APPENDIX A
THE TREASURE OF GOD'S WORD

I've searched through the treasure of God's Word in these months since Adrian went to heaven. Here are some of the treasures that I've found. I encourage you to read these verses over and over again. Then search for your own promises and mine your own treasures.

COMFORT

Blessed be the God and Father of our Lord Jesus Christ, the Father of mercies and God of all comfort, who comforts us in all our tribulation, that we may be able to comfort those who are in any trouble, with the comfort with which we ourselves are comforted by God. *(2 Corinthians 1:3–4)*

You shall weep no more. He will be very gracious to you at the sound of your cry; When He hears it, He will answer you. *(Isaiah 30:19)*

"Blessed are those who mourn, For they shall be comforted." *(Matthew 5:4)*

"For I will turn their mourning to joy, will comfort them, and make them rejoice rather than sorrow." *(Jeremiah 31:13)*

You, who have shown me great and severe troubles, shall revive me again, and bring me up again from the depths of the earth. You shall increase my greatness, and comfort me on every side. *(Psalm 71:20–21)*

This is my comfort in my affliction, For Your word has given me life. *(Psalm 119:50)*

GUIDANCE

The LORD will guide you continually, and satisfy your soul in drought, and strengthen your bones; you shall be like a watered garden, and like a spring of water, whose waters do not fail. *(Isaiah 58:11)*

For this is God, our God forever and ever; He will be our guide even to death. *(Psalm 48:14)*

Oh, send out Your light and Your truth! Let them lead me; let them bring me to Your holy hill and to Your tabernacle. *(Psalm 43:3)*

He makes me to lie down in green pastures; He leads me beside the still waters. He restores my soul; He leads me in the paths of righteousness for His name's sake. *(Psalm 23:2–3)*

For you are my rock and my fortress; therefore, for Your name's sake, lead me, and guide me. *(Psalm 31:3)*

The humble He guides in justice, and the humble He teaches His way. *(Psalm 25:9)*

The LORD is my shepherd; I shall not want. *(Psalm 23:1)*

Yea, though I walk through the valley of the shadow of death, I will fear no evil; for You are with me; Your rod and Your staff, they comfort me. *(Psalm 23:4)*

HEAVEN

And I heard a loud voice from heaven saying, "Behold, the tabernacle of God is with men, and He will dwell with them, and they shall be His people. God Himself will be with them and be their God. And God will wipe away every tear from their eyes; there shall be no more death, nor sorrow, nor crying. There shall be no more pain, for the former things have passed away." *(Revelation 21:3–4)*

But I saw no temple in it, for the Lord God Almighty and the Lamb are its temple. The city had no need of the sun or of the moon to shine in it, for the glory of God illuminated it. The Lamb is its light. *(Revelation 21:22–23)*

They shall see His face, and His name shall be on their foreheads. There shall be no night there: They need no lamp nor light of the sun, for the Lord God gives them light. And they shall reign forever and ever. *(Revelation 22:4–5)*

HELP

Our soul waits for the LORD; He is our help and our shield. For our heart shall rejoice in Him, because we have trusted in His holy name. *(Psalm 33:20–21)*

May the LORD answer you in the day of trouble; may the name of the God of Jacob defend you; may He send you help from the sanctuary, and strengthen you out of Zion. *(Psalm 20:1–2)*

As for God, His way is perfect; the word of the LORD is proven; He is a shield to all who trust in Him. *(Psalm 18:30)*

Our soul waits for the LORD; He is our help and our shield. For our heart shall rejoice in Him, because we have trusted in His holy name. *(Psalm 33:20–21)*

HOPE

And my God shall supply all your need according to His riches in glory by Christ Jesus. *(Philippians 4:19)*

He sent from above, He took me; He drew me out of many waters. *(Psalm 18:16)*

"Behold, I will do a new thing, now it shall spring forth; shall you not know it? I will even make a road in the wilderness and rivers in the desert." *(Isaiah 43:19)*

You are my hiding place and my shield; I hope in Your word. Uphold me according to Your word, that I may live; and do not let me be ashamed of my hope.
(Psalm 119:114, 116)

"The Lord is my portion," says my soul, "therefore I hope in Him!" . . . It is good that one should hope and wait quietly.
(Lamentations 3:24, 26)

LOVINGKINDNESS

Because your lovingkindness is better than life, my lips shall praise You. Thus I will bless You while I live; I will lift up my hands in Your name. *(Psalm 63:3–4)*

Hear me, O LORD, for Your lovingkindness is good; turn to me according to the multitude of Your tender mercies. *(Psalm 69:16)*

I will mention the lovingkindnesses of the LORD and the praises of the LORD, according to all that the LORD has bestowed on us, and the great goodness toward the house of Israel, which He has bestowed on them according to His mercies, according to the multitude of His lovingkindnesses. *(Isaiah 63:7)*

MERCY

But as for me, I will come into Your house in the multitude of Your mercy; in fear of You I will worship toward Your holy temple. *(Psalm 5:7)*

Have mercy upon me, O God, according to Your lovingkindness; according to the multitude of Your tender mercies, blot out my transgressions. *(Psalm 51:1)*

Though He causes grief, yet He will show compassion according to the multitude of His mercies. *(Lamentations 3:32)*

PEACE

I will both lie down in peace, and sleep; For you alone, O LORD, make me dwell in safety. *(Psalm 4:8)*

You will keep him in perfect peace, whose mind is stayed on You, because he trusts in You. Trust in the LORD forever, for in YAH, the LORD, is everlasting strength. *(Isaiah 26:3–4)*

And let the peace of God rule in your hearts, to which also you were called in one body; and be thankful. *(Colossians 3:15)*

For you shall go out with joy, and be led out with peace; the mountains and the hills shall break forth into singing before you, and all the trees of the field shall clap their hands. *(Isaiah 55:12)*

He shall enter into peace; they shall rest in their beds, each one walking in His uprightness. *(Isaiah 57:2)*

And the peace of God, which surpasses all understanding, will guard your hearts and minds through Christ Jesus.
(Philippians 4:7)

PRAISE

I will bless the LORD at all times; His praise shall continually be in my mouth. *(Psalm 34:1)*

But I will hope continually, and will praise You yet more and more. My mouth shall tell of Your righteousness and Your salvation all the day, for I do not know their limits. *(Psalm 71:14–15)*

Bless the LORD, O my soul; and all that is within me, bless His holy name! Bless the LORD, O my soul, and forget not all His benefits. *(Psalm 103:1–2)*

Bless the LORD, O my soul! O LORD my God, You are very great: You are clothed with honor and majesty. *(Psalm 104:1)*

I will praise You, O LORD, with my whole heart; I will tell of all Your marvelous works. *(Psalm 9:1)*

PRAYER

Save me, O God! For the waters have come up to my neck. *(Psalm 69:1)*

The LORD has heard my supplication; the LORD will receive my prayer. *(Psalm 6:9)*

The LORD is near to all who call upon Him, to all who call upon Him in truth. He will fulfill the desire of those who fear Him; He also will hear their cry and save them. *(Psalm 145:18–19)*

In my distress I called upon the LORD, and cried out to my God; He heard my voice from His temple, and my cry came before Him, even to His ears. *(Psalm 18:6)*

I will call upon the LORD, who is worthy to be praised; so shall I be saved from my enemies. *(Psalm 18:3)*

The LORD is righteous in all His ways, Gracious in all His works. The LORD is near to all who call upon Him, to all who call upon Him in truth. He will fulfill the desire of those who fear Him; He also will hear their cry and save them.
(Psalm 145:17–19)

I called on the LORD in distress; the LORD answered me and set me in a broad place. The LORD is on my side; I will not fear. What can man do to me?
(Psalm 118:5–6)

Seek the LORD while He may be found, call upon Him while He is near.
(Isaiah 55:6)

PROTECTION

The LORD is your keeper; the LORD is your shade at your right hand. The sun shall not strike you by day, nor the moon by night. *(Psalm 121:5–6)*

The LORD shall preserve you from all evil; He shall preserve your soul. The LORD shall preserve your going out and your coming in from this time forth, and even forevermore. *(Psalm 121:7–8)*

When you pass through the waters, I will be with you; and through the rivers, they shall not overflow you. When you walk through the fire, you shall not be burned. Nor shall the flame scorch you. For I am the LORD your God, the Holy One of Israel, your Savior *(Isaiah 43:2–3)*

There is no fear in love; but perfect love casts out fear, because fear involves torment. But he who fears has not been made perfect in love. *(1 John 4:18)*

For the Lord will not cast off forever. *(Lamentations 3:31)*

REFUGE

The LORD also will be a refuge for the oppressed, a refuge in times of trouble. *(Psalm 9:9)*

God is our refuge and strength, a very present help in trouble. . . . The LORD of hosts is with us; the God of Jacob is our refuge. Selah. *(Psalm 46:1, 7)*

From the end of the earth I will cry to You, when my heart is overwhelmed; lead me to the rock that is higher than I. *(Psalm 61:2)*

For in the time of trouble He shall hide me in His pavilion; in the secret place of His tabernacle He shall hide me; He shall set me high upon a rock. *(Psalm 27:5)*

A man will be as a hiding place from the wind, and a cover from the tempest, as rivers of water in a dry place, as the shadow of a great rock in a weary land. *(Isaiah 32:2)*

RESURRECTION

Knowing that He who raised up the Lord Jesus will also raise us up with Jesus, and will present us with you. For all things are for your sakes, that grace, having spread through the many, may cause thanksgiving to abound to the glory of God. Therefore we do not lose heart. Even though our outward man is perishing, yet the inward man is being renewed day by day. *(2 Corinthians 4:14–16)*

For we know that if our earthly house, this tent, is destroyed, we have a building from God, a house not made with hands, eternal in the heavens. For in this we groan, earnestly desiring to be clothed with our habitation which is from heaven. . . . So we are always confident, knowing that while we are at home in the body we are absent from the Lord. *(2 Corinthians 5:1–2, 6)*

But I do not want you to be ignorant, brethren, concerning those who have fallen asleep, lest you sorrow as others who have no hope. For if we believe that Jesus died and rose again, even so God will bring with Him those who sleep in Jesus. *(1 Thessalonians 4:13–14)*

SINGING

Because You have been my help, therefore in the shadow of Your wings I will rejoice. My soul follows close behind You; Your right hand upholds me. *(Psalm 63:7–8)*

But I will sing of Your power; yes, I will sing aloud of Your mercy in the morning; for You have been my defense and refuge in the day of my trouble. To You, O my Strength, I will sing praises; for God is my defense, my God of mercy.
(Psalm 59:16–17)

You shall have a song as in the night when a holy festival is kept, and gladness of heart, as when one goes with a flute, to come into the mountain of the LORD, to the Mighty One of Israel. *(Isaiah 30:29)*

Let the word of Christ dwell in you richly in all wisdom, teaching and admonishing one another in psalms and hymns and spiritual songs, singing with grace in your hearts to the Lord. *(Colossians 3:16)*

I will greatly praise the LORD with my mouth; yes, I will praise Him among the multitude. *(Psalm 109:30)*

STRENGTH

I will love You, O LORD, my strength. *(Psalm 18:1)*

I will go in the strength of the Lord GOD; I will make mention of Your righteousness, of Yours only. *(Psalm 71:16)*

My flesh and my heart fail; but God is the strength of my heart and my portion forever. *(Psalm 73:26)*

The LORD is my rock and my fortress and my deliverer; my God, my strength, in whom I will trust; my shield and the horn of my salvation, my stronghold. *(Psalm 18:2)*

My soul melts for heaviness; strengthen me according to Your word. . . . This is my comfort in my affliction, for Your word has given me life. *(Psalm 119:28, 50)*

He gives power to the weak, and to those who have no might He increases strength. Even the youths shall faint and be weary, and the young men shall utterly fall, but those who wait upon the LORD shall renew their strength; they shall mount up with wings like eagles, they shall run, and not be weary, they shall walk, and not faint. *(Isaiah 40:29–31)*

It is God who arms me with strength, and makes my way perfect. *(Psalm 18:32)*

The LORD is my light and my salvation; whom shall I fear? The LORD is the strength of my life; of whom shall I be afraid? *(Psalm 27:1)*

THANKSGIVING

Enter into His gates with thanksgiving, and into His courts with praise. Be thankful to Him, and bless His name. *(Psalm 100:4)*

Oh, give thanks to the LORD, for He is good! For His mercy endures forever. *(Psalm 107:1)*

Giving thanks always for all things to God the Father in the name of our Lord Jesus Christ. *(Ephesians 5:20)*

Be anxious for nothing, but in everything by prayer and supplication, with thanksgiving, let your requests be made known to God. *(Philippians 4:6)*

I will offer to You the sacrifice of thanksgiving, and will call upon the name of the LORD. *(Psalm 116:17)*

TRUST

Some trust in chariots, and some in horses; but we will remember the name of the LORD our God. *(Psalm 20:7)*

He trusted in the LORD, let Him rescue Him; let Him deliver Him, since He delights in Him! *(Psalm 22:8)*

But as for me, I trust in You, O LORD; I say, "You are my God." *(Psalm 31:14)*

Be merciful to me, O God, be merciful to me! For my soul trusts in You; and in the shadow of Your wings I will make my refuge, until these calamities have passed by. *(Psalm 57:1)*

VICTORY

He will swallow up death forever, and the Lord GOD will wipe away tears from all faces; the rebuke of His people He will take away from all the earth: for the LORD has spoken. *(Isaiah 25:8)*

The LORD your God, who goes before you, He will fight for you, according to all that He did for you in Egypt before your eyes. *(Deuteronomy 1:30)*

He sent from above, He took me; He drew me out of many waters. *(Psalm 18:16)*

"No weapon formed against you shall prosper, and every tongue which rises against you in judgment You shall condemn. This is the heritage of the servants of the LORD, and their righteousness is from Me," says the LORD. *(Isaiah 54:17)*

He bowed the heavens also, and came down with darkness under His feet. And He rode upon a cherub, and flew; He flew upon the wings of the wind.
(Psalm 18:9–10)

"These things I have spoken to you, that in Me you may have peace. In the world you will have tribulation; but be of good cheer, I have overcome the world."
(John 16:33)

For by You I can run against a troop, by my God I can leap over a wall.
(Psalm 18:29)

He calms the storm , so that its waves are still. Then they are glad because they are quiet; so He guides them to their desired haven. *(Psalm 107:29–30)*

And he said, "Listen, all you of Judah and you inhabitants of Jerusalem, and you, King Jehoshaphat! Thus says the LORD to you: 'Do not be afraid nor dismayed because of this great multitude, for the battle is not yours, but God's.'" *(2 Chronicles 20:15)*

WAITING ON GOD

I wait for the LORD, my soul waits, and in His word I do hope. My soul waits for the Lord more than those who watch for the morning—yes, more than those who watch for the morning. *(Psalm 130:5–6)*

Wait on the LORD; be of good courage, and He shall strengthen your heart; wait, I say, on the LORD. *(Psalm 27:14)*

Therefore the LORD will wait, that He may be LORD to you; and therefore He will be exalted, that He may have mercy on you. For the LORD is a God of justice; blessed are all those who wait for Him. *(Isaiah 30:18)*

Lead me in Your truth and teach me, for You are the God of my salvation; on You I wait all the day. *(Psalm 25:5)*

The LORD is good to those who wait for Him, to the soul who seeks Him. *(Lamentations 3:25)*

APPENDIX B
NAMES OF GOD
Comments by Adrian Rogers

Abba *(Daddy)*

Have you ever thought about God as a daddy? Galatians 4:6 says, "And because you are sons, God has sent forth the Spirit of His Son into your hearts, crying, 'Abba, Father!'"

Abba is the Aramaic word meaning "Daddy, Father." It's a term of warm affection, intimacy, and respect for one's father. Now, to some that may sound like an irreverent way to address God, but Jesus called God "Our Father" in Matthew 6:9 and He gave us that same right. In America, children call their fathers "Daddy." But in the Middle East, they say "Abba." Jesus says that we can call the great God of the universe, "Abba Father" . . . "Daddy Father."

Adonai *(Lord)*

The gifted violinist Fritz Chrysler had a Stradivarius violin that at one time belonged to an old Englishman. Chrysler offered to buy it, but the old man told him that the violin was not for sale.

One day he ventured to the old man's house and asked if he could touch it. The old man invited Chrysler in. He tucked it under his chin and began to draw the bow across the strings. Great tears began to well up in the old Englishman's eyes.

Chrysler saw the man's face and said, "I'm sorry, but I would so much like to buy this instrument."

The old Englishman said, "It is not for sale, but it is yours. You are the master. You alone are worthy of it."

When we call God *Adonai,* we are saying that He is the Master. He alone is worthy, nothing and no one else. He is worth all that we have and all that we are.

Alpha & Omega
(The Beginning and the End)

The noted historian H. G. Wells made a list of the ten greatest men of history, and number one on that list was Jesus Christ. But Jesus doesn't belong on that list. He doesn't belong on anybody's list. He is Jesus, the First and the Last.

Jesus said in Revelation, "I am Alpha and Omega." *Alpha* is the first letter of the Greek alphabet. *Omega* is the last. If Jesus was speaking to an English audience, He would say, "I am A and Z."

What Jesus is saying about the written Word is true about the living Word. John chapter one tells us that "In the beginning was the Word . . . and the Word became flesh, and dwelt among us." Jesus was in the beginning as the Word of God. And He is God's final word for all eternity.

Jehovah *(Lord)*

The name *Jehovah* is used some sixty-eight hundred times in the Bible. It is the personal covenant name of Israel's God. In the King James Version of the Bible, it's translated LORD God. Not only does it speak of God's strength, but also it speaks of the sovereignty of God and the goodness of God.

The root meaning of this name means "self-existing," One who never came into being, and One who will always be.

When Moses asked God, "Who shall I tell Pharaoh has sent me?" God said, "I AM THAT I AM."

Jehovah or Yahweh is the most intensely sacred name to Jewish scribes and many will not even pronounce the name. When possible, they use another name.

Jehovah Nissi *(The Lord, My Banner)*

The Lord is a reigning banner over us all the time. The Hebrew word for "banner" comes from the root word "to be high" or "raised." This was the name given to the altar that Moses erected to commemorate the defeat of the Amalekites at Rephidim (see Exodus 17:8–15).

He goes before us and behind us to give us the victory in all circumstances of life. Even in the midst of the battle, the banner of the Lord is raised over us.

Psalm 23:5 says, "You prepare a table before me in the presence of my enemies; You anoint my head with oil; my cup runs over."

Who is the God who prepares a table of celebration in the presence of the enemy? When the enemy shall come in like a flood, then shall the Lord hold up a banner before him. The victory in all of life is the Lord's.

Jehovah Rohi
(The Lord, My Shepherd)

Psalm 23 and John 10 are beautiful descriptions of God as our Shepherd, *Jehovah Rohi.* When we say, "Lord" we think of God's deity. When we say "my Shepherd," we think of God's humanity.

God in human form—Jesus Christ—prophesied in the Old Testament and revealed in the New Testament. The *Jehovah* of the Old Testament is the Jesus of the New Testament. As the Good Shepherd, He dealt with the penalty of sin. As the Great Shepherd, He deals with the power of sin. As the Chief Shepherd, He's coming to take us from the very presence of sin.

Jehovah Rapha *(The Lord, My Healer)*

Does Jesus heal? Yes! He is the Almighty Lord, our healer. He can heal instantaneously by a miracle. He can heal over time through medicine. But let me add, that not every saint will be healed in this lifetime either by miracle or by medicine, nor instantaneously or in time.

Right now God is more interested in having you holy rather than healthy. Our bodies are not yet redeemed. The redemption of the body is going to come at the rapture of the church and the resurrection of the Christian dead. It is at that time that we will be made like unto Him. There is no sickness in the Lord's body and there will be no sickness in our resurrection body. If you are not healed in this life, child of God, you will be healed in eternity.

Jehovah Shalom *(The Lord, My Peace)*

The Lord greeted Gideon in peace, so he built an altar and named it "The Lord is peace" (see Judges 6:23–24).

You have probably heard the blessing *Shalom* from Jewish friends and acquaintances. It means peace. More important, it means the Lord, our peace.

Where does the Shepherd lead His

sheep? Beside peaceful, still waters. "He makes me to lie down in green pastures; He leads me beside the still waters" (Psalm 23:2).

When your heart is content, you are at peace. And where does that contentment come from? The grace of God. There's no man more discontent than one who is not experiencing the amazing grace of God. Only in Jesus will you find security, sufficiency, and serenity.

Jehovah Shammah
(The Lord, Who Is There)

Psalm 139:7 asks, "Where can I go from Your Spirit? Or where can I flee from Your presence?" And what is the answer? God is omnipresent. He's everywhere.

Somebody said that God is a circle whose center is everywhere and whose circumference is nowhere. There is not a murmur, but that He hears it. There's not a movement, but that He sees it. There's not a motive, but that He knows it. Neither death, darkness, nor distance can hide us.

When I am discouraged, His presence sees me through. When I am lonely,

His presence cheers me up. When I am worried, His presence calms me down. When I am tempted, His presence helps me out.

Jehovah Saboath *(The Lord of Hosts)*

Jehovah Sabaoth literally means the LORD Almighty. It speaks of the sovereignty of God over all the powers of the universe.

David understood the greatness of God when he went against Goliath with five smooth stones and a sling. David said to Goliath, "Thou comest to me with a sword, and with a spear, and with a shield: but I come to thee in the name of the Lord of hosts, the God of the armies of Israel, whom thou hast defied" (1 Samuel 17:45).

Oh, that each of us would have this same conception of God in our battles.

Jehovah Tsidkunu
(The Lord, My Righteousness)

We are not righteous in and of ourselves. Our righteousness comes from God alone. Jesus imputes His righteousness into us so that we can see God. For you see, Hebrews 12:14 says that without holiness, "no one will see the Lord." Second Corinthians 5:21 says, "For He made Him who knew no sin to be sin for us, that we might become the righteousness of God in Him."

Isn't that terrific? You see, if you are a child of God, you are holy. Are you feeling that you can't live the Christian life? That's right where you need to be.

You see, God never asked you to live the Christian life apart from Him. He wants to be your strength. He wants to live the Christian life through you and do for you what you could never do for yourself.

Jehovah Jireh *(The Lord, My Provider)*

Jireh is from the same Hebrew word as *Moriah*, which is the name of the region where God sent Abraham to sacrifice Isaac (see Gen. 22).

In Genesis 22:11–13 we read, "But the Angel of the LORD called to him from heaven, and said, 'Abraham, Abraham!' So he said, 'Here I am.' And He said, 'Do not lay your hand on the lad, or do anything to him; for now I know that you fear God, since you have not withheld your son, your only son, from Me.' Then Abraham lifted his eyes and looked, and there behind him was a ram caught in the thicket by its horns. So Abraham went and took the ram, and offered it up for a burnt offering instead of his son."

God provided the lamb, and Abraham called the place *Jehovah Jireh*—God is our substitutionary sacrifice.